the ABCs of DISEASE MONGERING

THE ABCs of DISEASE MONGERING

AN EPIDEMIC IN 26 LETTERS

BY **Alan Cassels**

WITH RHYMES BY **Alisa Gordaneer**

ILLUSTRATIONS BY **Jeremy Gordaneer**

A POCKET POLICY PRIMER

FROM EMDASH PUBLISHING, VICTORIA, BC

Published by Emdash Book Publishing, Victoria, BC

Designed, printed and bound in Canada.

ℊ

Cassels, Alan, 1963 —

The ABCs of Disease Mongering: an epidemic in 26 letters. / by Alan Cassels.

ISBN 978-0-9780182-3-8

*To the many pharmaceutical
researchers, staff and executives
who develop needed drugs to
satisfy real disorders and not
simply shareholder greed.*

*And to the good doctors
in our midst
who prescribe those drugs
only when we need them.*

ACTIVE INGREDIENTS

ARE YOU
AT RISK?

ARE YOU AT RISK? No matter how healthy you might think you are, you're susceptible.

You're susceptible to an illness that's costing our health care system millions—even billions—every year.

It's so new it's only been recognized for a little more than a decade.

It's a disease that feeds on our ignorance and insecurities.

It could leave us poorer, in worse health, and dependent on more prescription drugs than we ever knew existed.

This disease is so insidious, it could attack even if you're watching for it.

It's a disease called . . . mongering.

The only cure is skepticism. To get your recommended dose, read on.

Diagnosis

WHAT IS disease mongering, anyway?

It's a condition caused by a dangerous combination of factors. Factors like the ability of well-funded medical science to develop new drugs. And the ability of those drugs to treat almost any condition.

It's fuelled by the need of corporations funding drug research to satisfy shareholders. And even more so, the ability of marketers working for drug companies to sell those innovative new drugs to everyone—even people who may not really need them.

There are other factors, too, like physicians who are pressed for time, consumers who are pressed for answers, and a society that is pressed to its limits in so many ways that it's no wonder we find ourselves vulnerable and demanding cures of all sorts.

IT'S EASY TO SEE WHY THE SELLING OF DRUGS— prescription pharmaceuticals designed to help us cope with all that ails us—is one seriously lucrative industry. Unfortunately, it's become as profitable as it is partly by amplifying our natural inclinations to want to treat every abnormality, ache, or worry that comes our way, even if the underlying cause has nothing to do with our body chemistry.

If we don't have an answer for why we're not feeling well, a new diagnosis or label may provide that needed sense of confirmation. Then, whatever prescribed remedy we are given—however irrational it might seem—justifies the disease. Sometimes those labels and treatments are a sound solution to our problems. Sometimes, however, they are just the beginning of more problems.

WE'RE ALL VULNERABLE TO DISEASE MONGERING, because it's a natural extension of our consumer culture, which would have us believe that consuming newer and better stuff is always the answer. But the irrational hyperconsumerism of disease mongering has turned the "pill for every ill" phenomenon on its head. In this case, an "ill for every pill" has now become the motivating axiom.

It's not only the patient or potential patient in all of us who is held in the grip of the disease mongers. Public health officials seem pressed to push vaccines beyond the evidence, and doctors can be so convinced of the benefits of drugs that most of their consultation with a patient is not about *whether* you'll get a prescription, but *which one* you'll get.

Even parents, desperate to raise healthy and well-adjusted children, can be convinced that a pharmaceutical answer to a perceived ailment in their kids is necessary, and many accept without question the simple chemical cure being offered.

In many ways, we're all innocent kids being offered simple, consumable solutions to a whole range of real and pseudo diseases, the treatment of which by pharmacotherapy is sometimes as wasteful as it is wrong-headed.

That's why the idea of this book was born. Because for every one of us, from Archie through Zoe, there's a new condition being created, moulded and shaped, mongered, sold, hawked and otherwise promoted in ways that are profoundly deceptive—yet utterly convincing.

The situation has become so astounding and absurd that there seemed only one way to point out just how absurd it is: a simple story, with 26 variations. There is a near-endless supply of new conditions to publicize, and new diseases to monger every day, but 26 examples should be enough to have anyone checking their blood pressure and pulse with at least a tad of concern.

IF YOU DOUBT WHETHER ANY OF THIS VERSE CAN BE BACKED UP BY FACT, CHECK OUT THE ENDNOTES ("The Fine Print"), where you'll find a note for every letter, with plenty of other research to sink your teeth into. Thankfully, there's a growing body of scholarly research that's gone into understanding how pharmaceutical markets are shaped, and how our attitudes are changing towards what is considered healthy and what is considered sick.

Of course, that doesn't mean the people who are truly suffering from any of the book's conditions or diseases are to be ridiculed. People at the extreme end need all the help they can get. And thankfully, many people can be well-served by the drugs referred to in this book. Still, it doesn't mean anyone who's told they're ill should take that news lying down.

Some might say the skepticism I'm offering is a particularly bitter pill to swallow—especially when we live in a world saturated with disease mongering—but that's why the subject needs this kind of touch. Even I believe it's best to sugar-coat things a little.

THAT'S THIS LITTLE BOOK. Take twenty-six letters. And think about whether you ought to call your doctor in the morning.

THE ABCs of DISEASE MONGERING*

* The "fine print" for each letter follows
the main text, beginning on page 65.

*Archie has Adolescent Motivational
Deficiency Disorder*

Archie's addicted to video games,
stuck on the couch—he's at it again!
His doctor says clearly Archie's just ill,
but AMDD can be cured by a pill.
But this evil disorder is really a joke—
it's such a tall order, I just had to poke.
(As if a small dose of Robophil*
could restore his flagging teen-age will.)
The diagnosis, you see,
    drives his poor parents crazy—
Archie's not sick, he's just plain old lazy.

* Trademarks referred to throughout this book
  are the property of their respective owners.

Ben has Bad Boy Behaviour

Ben is a brat, who just won't sit down.
He disrupts his schoolroom—
    he's such a class clown!
He's got a real thing–it's ADHD–
that merits a drug dose as fast as can be.
His brain, some think, is all in disorder—
and his lack of attention
    just won't come to order.
But drug companies love him,
    and his ADHD,
because the bigger the brats,
    the more profits they'll see.
(Even the grown-ups get in on the game,
with the same kinds of ills
    under more adult names.)

Carol is concerned about cholesterol

Carol takes capsules to curb cholesterol:
It's stuff in our blood that's essential to all.
Her doctor thinks hers, though,
    ain't such a good kind,
so Carol's got bad-lipid taming in mind.
She's pleased as punch now her levels are down,
but the truth of the matter
    makes some experts frown.
See, some skeptics question cholesterol drugs:
For women they're as useful as swallowing slugs.
They urge us to wonder, before opening wide,
what these substances do to our fragile insides.

Dennis desires to delay death

Dennis doesn't drink or smoke,
　　doesn't drive a car.
He lives his life quite carefully,
　　and never ventures far.
He thinks that he will never die,
　　he's absolutely sure,
as all the drugs he's taking
　　form a fundamental cure.
But the ones he takes to help his heart
　　could play hell with his liver,
and the ones for all his aches and pains
　　will set his heart a-quiver.
Too bad he doesn't read the stats,
　　or else he'd soon repent:
drugs don't ever defeat death—
　　the rate's one hundred per cent.

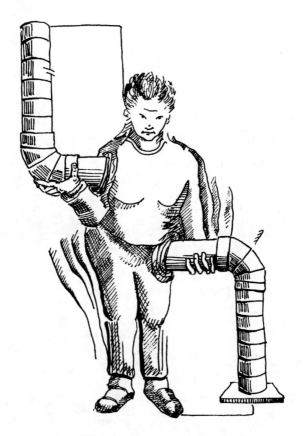

Ellen has estrogen deficiency

Ellen, poor Ellen, gets searing hot flashes,
with night sweats and mood swings
    and tears on her lashes.
Her doctor suggests that to stop her night pacing,
she augment her hormones—
    they just need replacing!
So she'll start on a regimen, it's called HRT,
and become vibrant and youthful—she'll feel 33!
She doesn't believe she's all that deficient,
but to dampen her flashes,
    drugs are nice and efficient.
(And guys, don't go thinking
    you don't need some, too—
testosterone's bound
    to make you spunky and new.)

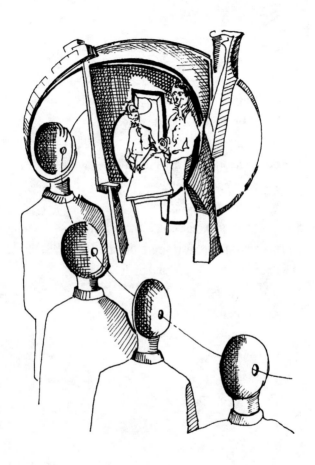

Ferdinand fears the flu

THE ABCS OF

What to do? What to do?
    Winter's here, and so's the flu!
Everyone across the land,
    just like our friend Ferdinand,
will roll up sleeves, and get in line,
    and pay for shots to keep them fine.
Nobody wants the chills and the aches,
or the dreaded bird flu—so, you do what it takes.
The flu mongers say, "It'll be a bad year,
get your shot in the arm,
    so you won't have to fear."
Of course, there's small proof
    that the shot does the trick.
Despite all the hassle, you *could* still get sick.

Gladys has high glucose

THE ABCS OF

Gladys is a sugar hound, Gladys likes her treats.
She doesn't want to change
    the way she eats and eats and eats.
Her doctor says her blood sugar
    is getting awful high—
if she doesn't take some insulin,
    he's worried she will die.
So Gladys gets herself a meter,
    does lots and lots of pricks—
but her "metabolic syndrome"
    is a metabolic schtick.
Now, Glad finds all these bloody tests
    make a fascinating hobby,
promoted to their utmost
    by a well-heeled pharma lobby.

Henrietta might catch the human
papillomavirus (HPV)

Henrietta's mother
    doesn't want a girl with warts,
'specially not down there,
    on her secret girly parts.
See, the HPV vaccine
    could save her cervix from some harm,
But her dad thinks through what it could mean—
    and he's growing quite alarmed.
Her parents just don't really know,
    they're caught in quite a tizzy—
Three shots to stop a long shot
    leaves them feeling rather dizzy.
But all the mongers say,
    in a manner quite polemic
that this shot is just the way
    to halt a future epidemic.

Ian has insomnia

THE ABCS OF

Ian has insomnia, Ian's counting sheep.
He's counted up to sixty-three,
    and he's still not going deep.
He wishes things were different,
    that he could just drift off . . .
but then he's woken, once again,
    as the baby starts to cough.
And then the neighbour's yappy mutt,
    and then his wife's sweet snore,
and then the clock blinks bleary red:
    it's quarter after four.
He begs his doc for a sleeping pill,
    to help him get some rest,
thus starting down a slippery slope,
    each prescription gets a test.
What happens in the end is sad,
    an obvious prediction:
Ian's still not sleeping well,
    and he's got a new addiction.

Jack has job-lock

THE ABCS OF

Poor Jack hates his job,
    an unpleasant position,
but he's locked in it due to
    some medical conditions.
(Every time his doctor
    dishes out another pill,
his insurance makes a note of it,
    as they calculate his bill.)
Jack would love to quit, you see,
    to break his job-lock chains,
but he becomes untouchable
    with all his aches and pains.
With each new diagnosis,
    Jack scores another label,
and thus his hopes for better work
    become ever more unstable.

Kevin has Kala Azar

THE ABCS OF

Corporal Kevin, in Kuwait, met a nasty fly.
It gave him Kala Azar, and now he's going to die.
His liver isn't doing well, and neither is his spleen—
so where are all the wonder drugs?
    Nowhere to be seen.
Guess a hundred thousand victims,
    dying in Sudan,
aren't quite enough a market
    for big pharma's research plan.
So forget about a cure, now, Kev,
    your soldier's bones are toast.
Are folks in R&D so blind
    to those who need them most?

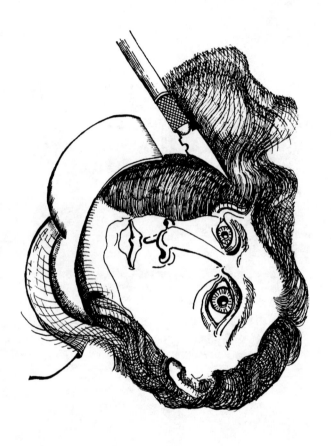

Laurel had laser eye surgery

THE ABCS OF

Laurel's corneas got the snip,
   Laurel's surgeon didn't slip.
Laurel's so happy to throw out her glasses
like millions of others—
   it's now done by the masses.
But peepers are precious, our peepers are gold,
and if corneal surgery just doesn't hold,
there are legions of lawyers about to get rich—
they prey on the surgeons
   who've had a small glitch.
So go Google "Laser,"
   "class action" and "eyes."
The wide range of lawsuits is quite a surprise.

Molly is menstruating

Molly's Aunt Flo is a nasty old type,
who monthly makes Molly so cranky, she gripes:
"If only I had a break once or twice—
why then, I might think
    that these monthlies were nice!"
So bring on the drugs
    for some menstrual suppression—
it'll give our dear Molly a happy expression.
Without her old cycles, she'll get lots more done—
and yes, she might score
    some more naughty-type fun.
But who really knows, when her cycle's disrupted
the ways her own functions
    could end up corrupted?
We don't have a clue,
    as no-one has studied
the long-term effects of those napkins unbloodied.

Norbert has narcolepsy

THE ABCS OF

Norbert isn't bored with you, he isn't even sad.
He's just got narcolepsy, and boy, he's got it bad.
He falls asleep when sitting,
    he snores when standing up.
Ol' Norbert loves his java,
    but he crashes in his cup.
He takes a drug, modafinil, to cure his sleepy fate,
but even so, he nods right off . . .
    at home, at work . . . on dates!
Norbert's case is different,
    he's one in just two grand,
but think about the market
    that's arising 'cross the land.
For every guy like Norbert
    there's two thousand late-night owls.
So, cue the infomercial!
    How the profiteers will howl!

Olive has osteoporosis

Olive O'Leary is getting so frail
she's turning to jelly as her bones start to fail.
Her doctor requested a machine diagnosis
to see if her bones harboured osteoporosis.
Her T-scores are low, she now fears a break,
so she's glad there's a treatment,
    which seems easy to take.
Disease mongers love Olives,
    they're old and they're scared.
In finding an illness, no test will be spared.
But poor Olive is losing to the mean Silent Thief—
and she clings to her drugs, for belief, not relief.

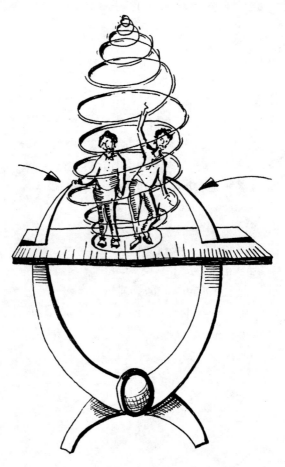

Peter and Paul are Pre-diseased

Two little boomers there, sitting on a wall:
Pre-Hypertension Peter, Pre-Diabetes Paul.
Of course the two aren't really sick,
    it hasn't come to that,
but as the two get older,
    something's sure to lay them flat.
So they go in for their frequent tests,
    for pokes and scans and measures.
They do it to preserve their health,
    despite the small displeasures.
They feel that they're now taking care, and
    standing on their guard.
When your body's only pre-diseased,
    it isn't all that hard.
Besides, they say, it's all a road
    that's paved with good intentions—
but an ounce or yes, a pound, of cure
    is worth billions in preventions.

Quinn has a quiescent tumour

THE ABCS OF

Quinn was on a noble quest,
    to find his perfect health.
He had about a million tests,
    befitting of his wealth.
When nothing told him anything,
    he tried to push his luck,
but doctors all just shook their heads,
    and ended up quite stuck.
He paid a thousand dollars
    to get a cat-scan answer:
they uncovered what he dreaded:
    a lump that could be cancer.
It didn't turn out all that bad;
    the lump was found benign—
better than the nasty bug
    he picked up at the time.
Quinn will tell you, now you ask,
    his awful tale of woe,
and remind you yes, that sometimes,
    it's better not to know.

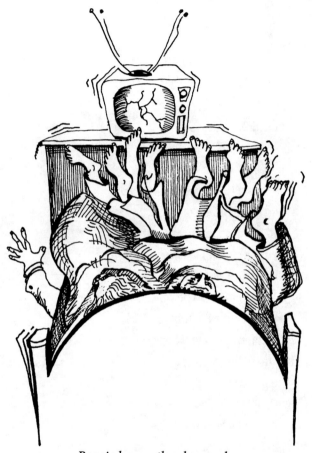

Reggie has restless leg syndrome

THE ABCS OF

Reggie's legs are restless,
    all twitchy in the night,
but his wife saw several TV ads
    for a drug to make them right.
She walked him to the clinic,
    to ask for some relief,
and he got a quickie look-over—
    it had never been so brief.
The doctor also knew the drug,
    and quickly wrote a script—
but next time, Reggie's wife says,
    the clinic he could skip.
She knew his troubles all along,
    and saw the right commercial.
Self-diagnosing illnesses?
    Why make it controversial?

Sue has social anxiety disorder

THE ABCS OF

Susan spilled her wine glass,
    Susan spilled some beer.
She dreads those office parties,
    which bring out all her fears.
She's got a strange new allergy,
    it seems she can't stand folks—
and thinks she hears the whispers
    as she's the butt of jokes.
Then Susan hears about a drug
    to cure her awful shyness,
and sails off to the clinic,
    for she's eager just to try this.
A few months later, there's our Sue,
    up dancing on the table.
She'll tell you all about her drug, but quit it?
    She's not able.
It took a lot for feisty Sue to come out of her shell,
but now she's so dependent
    that stopping would be hell.

Teddy has testosterone deficiency

Teddy has deficiency
    that robs his old vitality—
he clearly needs a supplement
    a "vitamin" called "T."
(He's grumpy and tired, he bellows and moans.
It means he's lacking testosterone.)
He gets a new cream to rub on his chest:
it brings back his libido, and his masculine best.
It perks up his mojo, it revs up his drive.
Makes him feel like he's just 25.
He gets more aggressive
    on this tough new regime,
but he feels much more manly
    with his script for some cream.

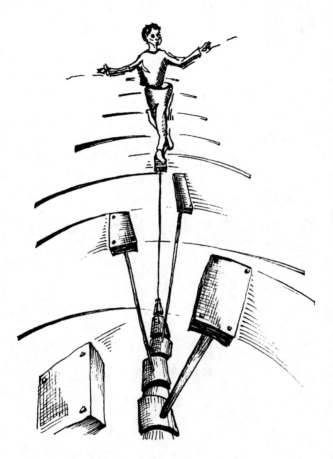

Ursula is undiagnosed

THE ABCS OF

Ursula isn't feeling great, she isn't feeling fine.
She isn't feeling poorly,
    but her health is on the line.
She's always waiting for results
    of tests and scans and probes,
certain that she's got the worst—
    but nothing ever shows.
She goes to see her doctor
    almost every single week,
convinced that something's wrong with her—
    but really she's a freak!
Don't ever give up, Ursula, don't ever let it rest.
Those who think they're well, it seems,
    just need to have more tests.

Veronica is really not that vain

THE ABCS OF

Veronica's lovely, but there's fuzz on her face—
Small furry bits that she'd like to erase.
Lucky for her, and her job on the news,
a nice drug called Vaniqa* can cure all her blues.
She won't have to live with that little moustache—
and if she reports out of Africa,
    she'll be glad of her stash.
Formulated first to cure sleeping sickness,
it also makes hair simply lose all its thickness.
Veronica's smooth face is the happy result—
and if she starts to get sleepy,
    she won't need a consult.

*Wilbert has a problem
with his Wee Willy*

THE ABCS OF

Alas for our poor Wilbert, whose willy is too fast.
He wishes he could be a man,
    and make it last and last.
His wife is getting irritated, and his girlfriend too—
so what's an eager guy like Willie ever gonna do?
He'll stand up proud and join the throngs
    of men around the nation,
who are happy for a label called
    Premature Ejaculation.
It sounds a bit more medical
    when you put that thought in motion—
and Willie won't be shy
    to ask his doctor for the potion.
(The side-effect will make him glad,
    his smile so incessant.
The pill for him will also work
    as a good ol' anti-depressant.)

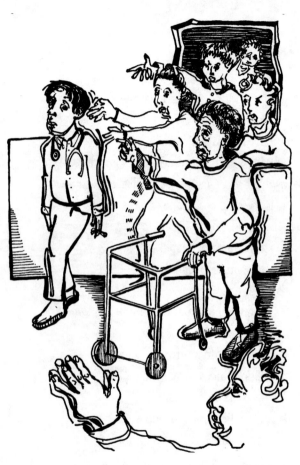

Xena takes Xanax

THE ABCS OF

Xena's taking Xanax* to help her with anxiety—
it comes up lots in company, and often in society.
But as much as she would like to feel
    a certain sweet relief,
the more she takes, the more she finds,
    it gives her way more grief.
See, all those drugs like Xena's pill—
    benzos, they are called—
can slowly lose their magic,
    until they're all but stalled.
But Xena keeps on taking them,
    because, as we predicted,
she and all her aging friends
    seem totally addicted.

Yolanda has yellow toenails

THE ABCS OF

Yolanda, Yolanda,
 she met a fine fellow—
how could she just tell him,
 her toenails are yellow?
She'd rather swallow something
 to clean up her feet,
than let her new romance
 go down in defeat.
So bring on terbinafine,
 it's sure to deliver ...
of course, it could also
 play hell with her liver.
But why should she care,
 for that goal of nice toes?
It's a risk that she takes,
 and her beau never knows.

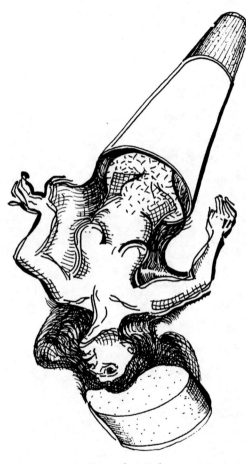

Zoe takes Zyban

THE ABCS OF

Zoe tried cold turkey, then she tried the patch,
but when it came to quitting,
  nothing was a match.
She knew she needed something
  to break that nasty habit—
so when her doctor offered Zyban*,
  she was sure she had to grab it.
Zoe isn't smoking now, in fact she's feeling fine—
bupropion is also found
  in the anti-depressant line.
Nice to know she's got a stone
  to kill two pesky birds—
but medicating habits still strikes us as absurd.
If someone ever makes a drug
  to package up willpower
we'll change our tune, and then we'll say,
  it's pharma's finest hour.

THE FINE PRINT

 Adolescent Motivational Deficiency Disorder (AMDD) is the only intentionally phony disease in the book. To make a point about how easy it was to create patients out of thin air, I created both AMDD and the pill Robophil*, and launched the pair on February 4, 2003, in a CBC radio documentary called "Manufacturing Patients."

The disease was later adapted by Australian researchers, recrafted into the adult version and launched as MoDeD (Motivational Deficiency Disorder) in the prestigious *British Medical Journal* on April Fool's Day, 2006—a report which was repeated, sometimes missing the joke, by major media outlets around the world. MoDeD, and the associated drug, Indolebant*, became the centerpiece of the world's inaugural conference on disease mongering in Newcastle, Australia, in April, 2006, featuring the researcher Dr. Leth Argos.

Healthfinder, a website of the United States Department of Health and Human Services, reported that "Indolebant is effective and well tolerated," and Argos said the drug worked so well, "one young man who could not leave his sofa is now working as an investment adviser in Sydney."

* Trademarks referred to throughout this book are the property of their respective owners.

THE FINE PRINT

B No one actually calls Attention Deficit/Hyperactivity Disorder (ADHD) "Bad Boy Behaviour," because it doesn't sound like a disease that could sell in the world of high-tech medicine. But someone's selling it: According to the journal *Health Affairs*, "global use of ADHD medications rose three-fold from 1993 through 2003," and other data show that about 10 million school children in the United States are currently diagnosed with ADHD.

The controversy around ADHD is real and sometimes explosive, with critics saying the growth in ADHD diagnoses in children is the result of a worsening social environment (insufficient physical exercise, too much junk food, overburdened classrooms and such), as well as defective science and pharmaceutical industry manipulation.

Could it really be true that currently more than a million kids in the U.S. are taking drugs because they can't sit still? There are no easy answers. A number of books are worth looking into. Fred Baughman and Crag Hovey's *The ADHD Fraud: How Psychiatry Makes "Patients" of Normal Children* debunks the medical orthodoxy around ADHD and highlights the very real dangers associated with diagnosing and drugging kids who are deemed hyperactive. Edward Hallowell and John Ratey's *Drive to Distraction* offers genuine methods to cope with ADHD. As for long-term use of ADHD drugs, the jury is still undecided. One Canadian meta-analysis published in the *Canadian Medical Association Journal* discusses this issue (Schachter et al, 2001).

Because cholesterol may be the most vivid illustration of the panoply of techniques used to monger disease, I and co-author Ray Moynihan made it the subject of the first chapter of our book *Selling Sickness*, entitled "Selling to Everyone."

Getting otherwise healthy people to swallow cholesterol propaganda depends on skillful fear-mongering. After all, who wouldn't want to avoid an early death from heart disease, if all you have to do is swallow a drug every day? An increasing number of people within the scientific community, however, aren't buying the cholesterol orthodoxy and are asking people to swallow it with a large swig of skepticism.

The International Network of Cholesterol Skeptics, made up of physicians and scientists around the world, attacks the cholesterol mongering head-on with some extremely cogent arguments against the world's current mania for cholesterol lowering.

Two books by members of the network are worth noting: Swedish scientist Uffe Ravnskov's *The Cholesterol Myths,* and the more recent work by British physician, Malcolm Kendrick, *The Great Cholesterol Con: The Truth About What Really Causes Heart Disease and How to Avoid It.*

Once you have sampled some of the forbidden fruit offered by the cholesterol skeptics, there's no going back. While there may be some benefits in lowering the cholesterol of high-risk men, the benefits don't extend to women. Despite the routine prescribing of statins to women, there is relatively good evidence that women don't benefit whatsoever from taking statin drugs (see Kendrick, *BMJ,* 2007). In terms of what these drugs do to our fragile insides, there are a range of side effects of statins, including amnesia. The most common problem seems to be myopathy or muscle-weakening, which is attributed the fact that statins deplete the body of a vitamin-like substance, Coenzyme Q10, needed for energy. Probably one of the most prolific writers on the side effects related to statins is a former NASA astronaut and physician named Duane Graveline. After experiencing statin-induced global transient amnesia himself, he began a journey through the medical literature and started writing books, including *Lipitor*—Thief of Memory.* In this, he explains in simple terms how the statins can alter brain function and memory, affect our muscles, and even cause psychiatric changes including disorientation, confusion and abnormal forgetfulness.

Don't get me wrong—for acute conditions, any drug that delays death is likely a good thing, as long as you can be sure its use will prolong your life and not shorten it due to unforeseen adverse reactions. However, in any decision to take a drug solely for prevention, the degree to which the drug may reduce your chances of dying from one cause has to be weighed against your chances of being harmed by the drug itself, or of accelerating your death by a different cause.

Many drugs treat symptoms, like the pain of arthritis, and such pain-relieving treatments make life more comfortable and worth living. At the same time, arthritis drugs have dangers, such as gastrointestinal bleeding. Many of us would gladly accept the trade-off of having our pain relieved despite the potential risk involved. But what remains problematic is that we often don't know the true dangers associated with drugs, and so can't make an informed decision over those trade-offs. For a drug like the infamous rofecoxib (Vioxx*), the slightly elevated risk of a heart attack or stroke might be worth the pain relief

THE FINE PRINT

it brings, but even physicians and specialists usually don't know what the full risks are, so even they can't fully advise a patient as to the dangers of the treatment.

An informative book about the scandal around Vioxx was recently published by Canadian doctors Christian Fortin and Jacques Beaulieu, entitled *Autopsie d'une catastrophe médicale—L'exemple du Vioxx*. The authors claim that the Vioxx debacle will revolutionize the pharmaceutical world. Bombastic words indeed. There may have been mini-skirmishes in the post-Vioxx era, but there has hardly been anything one would call "revolutionary" happening in terms of massive improvements in patient safety. It is, unfortunately, *caveat emptor* when you are deciding whether to swallow that new pill or not.

 One of the most startling drug-related discoveries made recently is the huge health benefit related to women stopping a drug treatment. That doesn't happen very often, so when it does, we sit up and take notice. At the end of 2006, scientists announced a large drop in new cases of breast cancer rates in the United States, based on a trend analysis of U.S. federal cancer statistics. They revealed that breast

cancers declined by 7.2 per cent in 2003, the year after large numbers of women stopped taking estrogen for menopause. The Women's Health Initiative study, which was halted in July, 2002, warned that estrogens taken for menopause resulted in a higher risk of breast cancer, heart disease and other problems.

Was this dip in numbers caused by millions of women stopping the estrogen and progestin pills they were taking? It's still not clear, but that seems to be the prevailing way of explaining why about 14,000 fewer women than expected were diagnosed with the disease.

A compelling and engaging book written about the creation and marketing of hormone replacement therapy is Barbara Seaman's *The Greatest Experiment Ever Performed on Women: Exploding the Estrogen Myth*. Gloria Steinem hailed Seaman as the "first prophet of the women's health movement," and goes on to note, "her prophecies are still coming true."

If you have any preconceptions around menopause mongering, you should definitely check out this book.

F Challenging the annual flu vaccine may be like discrediting mothers' milk. The annual flu campaigns have become so ingrained that it is difficult for people to be skeptical about the shot, even when some serious critical thinking is in order.

I started being skeptical when I found the scientific rationale for the annual flu shot wasn't that great. For the best information on whether a health intervention works, you shouldn't just look at one study, but rather examine an overview, or meta-analysis, of all the good quality studies you can find.

The Cochrane Collaboration is an international not-for-profit and independent organization, dedicated to making up-to-date, accurate information about the effects of healthcare readily available worldwide. This organization gathers and synthesizes all available medical literature, and in the case of the flu shot in healthy people, the reviewers examined 38 clinical trials, involving 66,248 healthy people, on the effectiveness, efficacy and harms of influenza vaccines. Their conclusion gives one pause for thought: "There is not enough evidence to decide whether routine vaccination to prevent influenza in healthy adults is effective."

Elderly people might benefit slightly more, especially those who live in long-term care facilities. But for healthy working people who are getting the flu shot to avoid missing work in the winter, the benefits are modest indeed.

The Cochrane review goes on to say that even though the vaccine works against the virus about 80 per cent of the time (as confirmed by lab tests), and that it works against "influenza-like" illness 30 per cent of the time, it made little difference in terms of the number of people going to hospital or experiencing complications, which to me would be the marker of an effective flu campaign. It added that "some vaccines cause pain and redness at the site of injection, muscle ache, and other very rare serious harms, such as transient paralysis."

 According to the World Health Organization, the world's population of people with type-2 diabetes in 2000 was approximately 171 million, a number predicted to double to more than 366 million by 2030. Type-2 diabetes is what used to be called adult-onset diabetes, as opposed to type-1, which often develops in youth and requires daily insulin shots to treat.

While type-2 diabetes is a dreadful disease that

can often end in amputations, blindness and an early death, there is perhaps no better example of rampant profit-driven disease mongering than the flurry of activity that happens around selling assorted diabetes paraphernalia—drugs, glucose testing meters and insulin—to treat type-2 diabetics. Much needs to happen to reduce the global burden of diabetes, but it is clear the mongering of our blood sugar is fueling a market that, in 2005, was worth about $18.6 billion. According to a 2007 report by Epscom Business Intelligence called *Diabetes Drug Discoveries: What the Future Holds*, the revenue from diabetes drugs will climb 50 per cent by 2011, and the "global market for diabetes therapy is expected to top $31 billion within the next five years."

Many of the problems of type-2 diabetes can be solved by losing weight, but there seems to be insufficient appetite for doing anything serious about weight-loss, simply because there's too much money in fat people. The writer Thomas Goetz notes in his *Wired Magazine* article entitled "The Thin Pill," that the drug industry has unequivocally fuelled obesity mongering, most noticeably in the creation and promotion of metabolic syndrome. It is Goetz's contention that Big Pharma has turned obesity into a disease, then invented the drugs to cure it.

This is further confirmed in an interview with Dr. Victor Montori, who was a lead author of a *British Medical Journal* analysis of a trial meant to determine the effectiveness of two drugs in treating type-2 diabetes. Montori criticized the current mania for treating diabetics with drugs, saying: "If I do nothing, 25 per cent of [high-risk] people will [eventually] need a drug. And instead of letting them find out who that 25 per cent is, I give it to 100 per cent of my patients. No obvious benefit. Clear waste of societal resources. And a distraction from a clear message of lifestyle changes." He goes on to describe the cascade effect of giving drugs to people who have mild blood glucose problems: "Pills beget blood tests to make sure the pills are not causing trouble, or to monitor the effect of this, and more doctor visits to look over the results of those tests and see how you're doing. All of a sudden, you become a patient. And up until that point . . . you're just a healthy person at risk of a disease." Extolling the adverse effects of all this diabetes mongering, he says this activity: "clogs waiting lists [with] people that are essentially well but are worried because they now have a diagnosis or they're taking a tablet. And so, gosh, in a system that is struggling to make ends meet—which in other words defines any healthcare system in the world—to have these extra costs in people that are otherwise healthy appears foolish."

Two things would really kill the massive spending on type-2 diabetes paraphernalia like blood test strips, monitors, drugs and insulins: exercise and healthier diets. Researchers like Ruth Colagiuri and colleagues, publishing in the *Australian Journal of Public Health*, argue that social policy, such as changes to our social and physical environments—and not obsession with altering blood glucose—is what's really needed to reduce the incidence and prevalence of diabetes.

Research on the influence of better diets is growing as well. One recent book, Dr. Neal Barnard's *Program for Reversing Diabetes: The Scientifically Proven System for Reversing Diabetes Without Drugs* cites studies funded by the National Institutes for Health showing a well-balanced, largely vegan diet can control blood sugar three times more effectively than the diet recommended by the American Diabetes Association. When I spoke to him, Dr. Barnard said for most people, better eating will improve the body's ability to respond to insulin and even reverse the symptoms of diabetes. This, of course, is heresy to the diabetes mongers hoping to cash in on that $31 billion worth of drugs and other diabetes stuff entering the marketplace.

On July 18, 2006, Canada approved the use of Gardasil*, a vaccine to prevent cervical cancer caused by the human papillomavirus (HPV). Merck, the manufacturer, is allowed to market the vaccine for girls and women ages nine to 26, a decision that, on its own, is rife with controversy. Using a vaccine in the wider general population to prevent a disease transmitted by sexual contact, and for which there is a proven screening protocol (the PAP smear), raises oodles of moral, legal and medical questions.

The key challenge in marketing this vaccine is that it requires parents to be convinced that they need to get their young daughters vaccinated for a sexually transmitted virus long before these girls are likely to be sexually active.

While Gardasil's importance in preventative medicine is still unknown, the hullabaloo around it may foreshadow coming controversies. Researchers creating cancer vaccines face the annoying fact that cancer often develops over many years, even decades, and probably is caused by a mix of genetic, lifestyle and environmental causes. No one really knows if it is even possible to develop immunity to a disease that may take decades to grow. There are many unknowns about vaccinating to prevent HPV, and it is largely those unknowns which have kept the controversy alive. Is it possible we might inoculate millions of girls with hundreds of millions of dollars worth of vaccines, only to trade the risk of one kind of death for the risk of another?

McGill University epidemiologist Abby Lippman and colleagues wrote a commentary in the *Canadian Medical Association Journal* on the questions around Gardasil after the Canadian government announced a $300 million federal fund to help the provinces set up HPV vaccination programs which stirred up a hornets' nest of controversy which can be read at the

CMAJ online site. For further information about the safety of vaccines, check out the National Vaccine Information Centre in the U.S. at: www.nvic.org.

Q There are a range of prescription sleeping pills, no matter what kind of insomnia you might have. And while there are no prescription sleeping pills approved for treating annoyingly sleepless infants, that doesn't stop physicians from prescribing whatever treatment they want to any patient they think would benefit from it. In the United States, Ambien* (zolpidem tartrate), Lunesta* (eszopiclone), and Sonata* (zaleplon) dominate the sleeping pill market, with marketing ploys that highlight the individual drug's special ability to treat a different insomniac sub-type. The underlying theme is that these drugs are "safer" and characterized as not addictive—unlike the older benzodiazepine drugs formerly used to treat sleeping disorders. As far as I know, there are currently no approved sleeping pills free of the dangers of addiction. However, people with sleep problems should know that if they start down the road of solving sleep problems with pills, they could find themselves both addicted to the treatment and with other sleep-related problems on their hands.

Some truly bizarre forms of sleep-related behaviors have been reported in people who take insomnia drugs, including sleep driving—driving while not fully awake after taking a sleeping pill—and sleep eating.

A key marketing trick used to convince many of us that pharmaceutical enhancement is needed for sleep problems is the handy little self-diagnostic "Sleep IQ" quiz. For example:

> ❏ *Do you watch the late show because you can't fall asleep?*
> ❏ *Are you often cranky?*
> ❏ *Do you eat spicy foods for dinner?*
> ❏ *Do you experience a lot of stress in your life?*

If you answer "yes" to a couple of those, you're set to become a new patient for one of these drugs. The punch line of any self-diagnostic quiz, by the way, is the extremely predictable, disease-mongering mantra: "See your doctor." No one else has the power to send you to sleep heaven with a "safe," monitored, prescription drug. Rather than marketing more pills, people need to be sold on the idea of improving their "sleep hygiene," by adopting a series of behaviours that contribute to better sleep.

One prominent voice warning us about the dangers of sleeping pills is Daniel F. Kripke, a physician and professor of psychiatry at the University of

California, San Diego. He has an online book called *The Dark Side of Sleeping Pills,* available at www.darksideofsleepingpills.com.

J As a phenomenon, "Job Lock" is mainly worrisome in the United States, where people get health insurance coverage through their employers—but you'll also find it in Canada if you try to seek private or extended health insurance. Job Lock is not a disease, exactly, but for many people it's a condition that consists of a diagnosis placed in your permanent medical file for a reason—legitimate or not—that remains there even when the reason for the original diagnosis may have passed.

When people start to learn—usually when they're turned down for additional health coverage—that past diagnoses may rise up, zombie-like, to haunt them, they may be much more reticent to visit their doctor. Because Job Lock is caused by the detritus you may have accumulated in your personal medical records, you'll want to be particularly careful in allowing diagnoses of pseudo- or mongered diseases to be applied to you. It's hard to unstick a diagnosis that has stuck.

 When soldiers like Corporal Kevin travel to foreign countries and get local diseases that aren't a problem back home, they may be unwittingly stimulating a market for drug development. There's no room for mongering when there are no buyers, but that equation sometimes changes when our armed forces get sent into the fray. Sending soldiers abroad has a history of helping to drive research for treatments for infectious diseases that exist primarily in poor countries.

For example, some of the early treatments for malaria, one of the world's most serious killers, came out of the American and French experiences of Vietnam, where soldiers were exposed to this dangerous disease. Time will tell if American or NATO involvement in Afghanistan, Kuwait or Iraq will eventually deliver essential medicines for diseases such as Kala Azar—both for the people who live there, and the troops who are just visiting. Some groups, such as the Institute for OneWorldHealth and Médecins Sans Frontièrs' Drugs for Neglected Diseases Initiative are developing novel therapies for diseases such as Kala Azar, but the lack of substantial commercial return means the flow of capital to fund the development of these sorely needed treatments is only a trickle.

THE FINE PRINT

 LASIK, which stands for laser-assisted in situ keratomileusis, involves a surgeon reshaping a patient's cornea with a computer-calibrated laser. It is the most common elective surgery in the United States, with millions of procedures done every year. It's very quick, and when it is effective, many people swear by it. But like any new technology, especially one where the potential dangers haven't been spelled out, or there is huge commercial pressure to move patients through quickly, the complaints and problems start to appear.

There are a range of adverse effects, or complications, that affect somewhere between three and six per cent of people who undergo the surgery. Some of the complications include slipped flap, corneal infection, haziness, and halo or glare, and some are irreversible. There are websites established to help people rehabilitate from problems with laser eye surgery, such as the Vision Surgery Rehab Network.

Part of the problem with the commercialism of any medical procedure is the practitioners' tendency to cut corners to beat out competitors. LASIK surgery is practiced in the private sphere, and is sold in a highly competitive way, sometimes employing hard-sell advertising, price wars, and poor screening of potential candidates.

 **M** Following a 2003 survey of consumer and health professional attitudes toward suppressing periods, conducted by the Association for Reproductive Health Professionals, the lead author, Linda Andrist said: "women and health care providers in this study thought that menstruation is a natural event and should not be treated like a disease; however, having the choice of not menstruating every month appears to be an intriguing option for women."

This "intriguing option" points to a market of growing importance for manufacturers like Barr Laboratories, which makes Seasonique*, a drug that reduces the number of periods from 13 to four per year.

Wonder if your doctor is getting the straight goods on menstrual suppression? Here's how Barr Labs describes its sales activities in the U.S.: "The Duramed sales forces promote Seasonique to approximately 40,000 physicians and other healthcare providers in the United States. Marketing support includes professional education materials, published data from our clinical studies demonstrating the safety and efficacy of the extended-cycle concept, and product sampling kits that contained extensive information for patients. Detailing activities are reinforced with a trade-advertising program in leading medical journals and Direct-To-Consumer ("DTC") advertising."

Susan Rako, the author of *No More Periods?: The Risks of Menstrual Suppression and Other Cutting-Edge Issues About Hormones and Women's Health* describes it this way in her book: "Tampering with the hormonal climate of healthy menstruating women, including teenage girls whose lives stretch ahead for decades, for the purpose of doing away with their periods is, in a word, reckless. Manipulating women's hormonal chemistry for the purpose of menstrual suppression threatens to be the largest uncontrolled experiment in the history of medical science. Hands down."

N The need to stay awake in a busy world has kept the anti-sleep drug market buoyant, and growing, with modafinil (which also goes by the names Provigil*, Alertec*, Vigicer*, etc.) now being used to treat narcolepsy, obstructive sleep apnea, excessive daytime sleepiness and "shift work sleep disorder."

The off-label (unapproved) uses are growing too, and people take it for everything from cognitive

THE FINE PRINT

enhancement (some call it a "smart" drug), as a treatment for amphetamine addiction, as a doping agent for high performance athletes, for relief from the symptoms of multiple sclerosis, and to treat the sleepiness that comes with the treatments for ADHD.

It is especially famous for its military applications, and has been used by the French Foreign Legion, U.S. army helicopter and fighter pilots, and even tested in ground forces, where it apparently didn't do much better than good old coffee. A comparison with caffeine, published in 2002, said one dose of modafinil was equal to about 600 mg of caffeine, in terms of improvements in performance and vigilance. (Drip coffee contains about 110–175 mg of caffeine, so you'd have to drink about four cups to get that same jolt.) However, as it's currently retailing in the U.S. for about $7–8 per one 200 mg pill, modafinil might be slightly cheaper than an equivalent amount of cappuccino.

O After looking at this condition for more than ten years, I have one request: "Can someone please tell me something about osteoporosis that *isn't* controversial?"

The very definition of the disease (which drug

makers had a hand in shaping), the usefulness of the bone density test, the need for caution in how you swallow the drug, the safety of those drugs, and the very modest overall health impact of treating osteoporosis as a disease in the first place, are all subjects of intense and heated controversy.

Women are scared stiff of osteoporosis, largely because they are led to believe that having it will lead to a hip fracture, which will most certainly lead to an early death. The prognosis is not great for many elderly women experiencing a hip fracture, so this fear is understandable. But if they knew the very minimal help osteoporosis drugs provide, they wouldn't go swallowing their doctors' advice as fast as they do.

There is good research on the effects of exercise, such as tai chi and yoga, in preventing hip fractures. It seems to work, particularly because these types of exercise strengthen coordination and balance, which in turn can prevent falls. Another way is to avoid other drugs, particularly benzodiazepines (see letter X), which can cause dizziness and falls.

When offered osteoporosis drugs, people should ask their doctors the NNT question. NNT stands for numbers-needed-to-treat, and most doctors prescribing drugs for prevention should be able to tell how many patients would have to be treated to prevent one "event," such as a heart attack or, in the case of osteoporosis, a hip fracture.

While women may mightily fear osteoporosis, the NNT figure, obtained from various reviews, such as an excellent one produced by the Canadian Agency for Drugs in Technology and Health, said that to avoid a *single* hip fracture "event," a doctor would have to treat 943 women aged 55 to 59 for five years with 10 mg of alendronate daily. The drug is also called Fosamax* and is available in generic form at the price of about $1.76/day. That's a whole lot of drugs taken by an awful lot of women just to prevent one fracture, and it's not exactly the easiest drug in the world to take. Due to its corrosive nature, alendronate is linked to severe and permanent damage to the esophagus and stomach. Its other known side effects include diarrhea, flatulence, rashes, headaches and muscular pain.

Imagine the cost and potential side effects of treating nearly 1,000 women for five years with such a drug. Furthermore, the NNT changes depending on the outcome you're looking for. If a doctor prescribes alendronate to reduce vertebral fractures, another common risk of osteoporosis, it would have to be for 15 women for three years to prevent *one* vertebral fracture. These fractures are often asymptomatic (you don't feel them) but are one of the reasons people get shorter with advanced age—their vertebrae slowly collapse. See the University of Toronto Centre for Evidence-Based Medicine for many good examples of NNT in a variety of conditions. For a fascinating book exposing the controversies around osteoporosis, check out Gillian Sanson's *The Myth of Osteoporosis: What every woman should know about creating bone health.* Any woman who has been told she has osteoporosis or its little sister, osteopenia, should head to the library or bookstore and get this New Zealander's excellent book.

P The "pre-disease" phenomenon allows the disease-mongering net to spread even wider, capturing new customers beyond the boundaries of what were previously considered traditional, treatable diseases. In terms of high blood pressure, even the conservative *Harvard Medical School Family Health Guide* says "Prehypertension is not an illness—but it is an important warning that illness lies ahead." Knowing you are "prehypertensive" (with a blood pressure of anywhere from 120/80 to 129/89) might motivate you to improve your diet or lose some weight. However, is it possible there is far too much hypertension mongering going on?

In terms of "prediabetes," according to the *Pharmaceutical Journal's* POEM (Patient-Oriented Evidence that Matters) entitled: *Treating prediabetes does not affect progression,* "there is no clear and absolute benefit in identifying and treating people with prediabetes." Like many "pre" diseases, prediabetes is clearly a bid to get people onto treatment long before they exhibit any symptoms. You can see why it makes a compelling argument for treating milder forms of conditions: "Why not prevent the fire instead of waiting until it starts?" Yet, like much of what passes for preventive strategy, the whole screening and testing phenomenon is not well studied. Therefore, it is impossible to say with any certainty if all this diabetes mongering is having a net positive effect.

In terms of "pre-hypertension," the Therapeutics Initiative at the University of British Columbia covered the issue of when to treat "mild hypertension," and stressed an important point: at the end of the day, it's up to the patient to ultimately decide whether or not they want to medicate their blood pressure. Like any drug, a patient needs ti be provided information that clearly outlines the benefits and harms of any proposed treatment. Amen.

Q Diagnostic fishing expeditions carried out by the medical screening professions need some serious lay explanations. Otherwise, growing numbers of people will continue to rush out for useless and potentially harmful screening tests. Thankfully, there's a great book in this area, H. Gilbert Welch's *Should I be Tested for Cancer: Maybe Not*

and Here's Why. It is a most readable account of the controversies and uncertainties around screening, and certainly blows the lid off of the "screen early, screen often" creed that has gripped our medical system and has infected our collective consciousness.

The Centre for Medical Consumers, an independent source of health and drug information based in New York City, has looked closely at the risks of the full-body scan, which they say has been "heavily promoted to the public as a means of finding cancer before symptoms appear." As with any new screening technology, the test could show both false positives and false negatives, and patients could be led to think they're not as sick as the doctors say, or, conversely, are possibly not as healthy as they themselves might think.

Screening from computed tomography (CT) scans is problematic, especially when they are done on essentially healthy people. The radiation doses delivered by these tests are actually of sufficient intensity to *cause* cancer. You don't have to look hard to find the detractors dishing out cautions around the newest screening technologies. The relatively conservative FDA Center for Devices and Radiological Health says the use of CT scans to screen people free of symptoms is of "no proven benefit."

 **R** Like many new diseases or conditions, Restless Legs Syndrome is very real for many people, but the prevalence is exaggerated so as to capture a much wider pool of potential patients. Do 30 million Americans really have restless legs? Sound fanciful?

The website put out by Glaxo-Smith Kline, the manufacturer of the first drug approved to treat this new syndrome (Requip*), asks the typical disease-mongering questions: "Are your legs keeping you up at night? Do you dread long business meetings, going to the movies, or traveling on an airplane because you know your restless legs won't let you sit still? You just know you'll have to get up to relieve the discomfort in your restless legs—disturbing your work colleagues, other moviegoers, and fellow passengers. If this sounds familiar, you may have Restless Legs Syndrome (RLS), which includes mild, moderate, and severe symptoms and affects approximately one in 10 adults in the U.S.. RLS is a common medical condition characterized by an uncontrollable urge to move the legs when sitting or lying down."

So one in ten of us has restless legs? Like most disease mongering, the drive to exaggerate the prevalence, or the size of the patient population, is designed to normalize the condition. The main problem is that when we let the marketers tell us how big the market is, without independent and objective information to verify these data, we are left to the machinations of the mongers. For a good chuckle, you might want to look for an online spoof on YouTube, entitled "Restless Penis Syndrome."

Restless Leg Syndrome is so widely marketed in television and magazine advertising that it has become the laypersons' most commmonly recognized example of disease mongering.

S Barry Brand, the product director for Paxil*, was quoted on June 26, 2000, in the journal *Advertising Age* saying: "Every marketer's dream is to find an unidentified or unknown market and develop it. That's what we were able to do with social anxiety disorder."

The public relations company Cohn and Wolfe, which led Paxil's early marketing efforts, won major advertising awards for its work in expanding this relatively unknown condition, using celebrities, direct-to-consumer advertising and media relations. How do you shape medical and public opinion about disease? The answer appeared in *Pharmaceutical Marketing*, one of the drug industry's key publications directed at marketing executives. The author used the promotion of social phobia as the best example.

On the other side, Charles Medawar's UK group, Social Audit, has probably led the English-speaking world in exposing the problems with antidepressants in general. Referring to paroxetine (the generic name for Paxil or Seroxat*), he told the *British Medical Journal* in 2002 that "this drug has been promoted for years as safe and easy to discontinue [but] the fact that it can cause intolerable withdrawal symptoms of the kind that could lead to dependence is enormously important to patients, doctors, investors, and the company."

Those interested in the clandestine world of antidepressant drug regulation and promotion should check out Medawar's book (co-written with Anita Hardon), *Medicines out of Control?—Antidepressants and the Conspiracy of Goodwill*. For a longer analysis about the making of social anxiety disorder, check out Christopher Lane's *Shyness: How Normal Behavior Became a Sickness*. The subject is also examined, albeit in an abbreviated form, in chapter seven of Ray Moynihan and Alan Cassels' *Selling Sickness: How the World's Biggest Pharmaceutical Companies are Turning us All into Patients*.

THE FINE PRINT

 Ads for the testosterone drug Andriol* encourage doctors to ask their largely older male patients if they are tired, moody, or have low sexual interest. The ads' tagline says it all: "Getting old is natural. The goal . . . to make feeling old optional."

Let's face it, guys, most of us lose our mojo as we age, making the disease mongers rub their hands with glee at such a large potential market. Toronto family physician Dr. Catherine Oliver told the *Toronto Star* she "cringes at the sight of medical journals that arrive in the office with full-page colour ads from drug companies urging doctors to prescribe testosterone for andropause in older male patients." The *Star* article, describing various diseases being mongered in Canada, likened the issue with men and andropause to essentially a "remake of the hormone replacement therapy scare that had millions of menopausal women taking the treatment until independent studies released in 2002 found they can increase the risk of cancer and heart disease."

In studies, the most common side effects reported for men using AndroGel* were abnormal lab tests, acne, prostate disorders, skin irritation, gynecomastia (abnormally large breasts), and impaired urination.

 Hypochondria has been around for a long time, and people have been slagging hypochondriacs just as long. The appearance of hypochondria in literature has many colorful examples, one of the most famous being the French author Jules Romain's popular play *Knock, ou le triomphe de la médecine*. In this comedy, Romain satirizes the hypochondria of rural villagers when a young, suave physician, with his modern equipment and fancy medical language, dupes an entire town into thinking they are suffering from a cornucopia of strange illnesses.

The rise of direct-to-consumer advertising of pharmaceuticals in the U.S., a phenomenon that has grown from essentially zero in 1996 into a $6 billion-per-year industry in 2007, is probably the world's largest corporate-sponsored hypochondria epidemic ever seen. The average American consumer is exposed to ten drug ads on TV every day, asking "Do you have restless legs?"; "Do you sometimes feel sad?"; "Do you have trouble falling asleep?" and so on, all while urging viewers to see their doctors for the elixirs to combat these illnesses. Nothing characterizes disease mongering better than pitching the diseases and the remedies straight to the intended audience, and bypassing doctors.

V For the 2003 CBC radio documentary "Manufacturing Patients," I interviewed Daniel Berman, coordinator of the Access to Essential Medicines Campaign based in Geneva, Switzerland, about the prescription medication Vaniqa*.

Here's what he said:

> "It is an incredible story, and there is a level of serendipity to it, because the medicine for sleeping sickness, eflornithine, was completely out of production, and then suddenly a new drug with the same active ingredient burst onto the scene. And when I say burst onto the scene, in the U.S. there were television advertisements; women's magazines like *Glamour*, or *Vanity Fair*, had five-six page advertisements for this drug, and the new formulation, or the new drug—well, it's not a new drug, it's a new use for an old drug—was to remove facial hair on women. And so here, the companies Bristol-Meyers Squibb and Gillette had developed this new indication and done clinical trials and were aggressively marketing that product. Now, that was great news for people with sleeping sickness, because it gave us the leverage with the companies."

He went on to describe how his organization created a public relations near-disaster when it took the story to the *New York Times,* making the link between Vaniqa and eflornithine for sleeping sickness. That's what it took for the company to promise to start producing the drug in a form meant to be used by the poor of Africa.

Three major epidemics of sleeping sickness have occurred in the past century, affecting tens of thousands of people in sub-Saharan Africa.

In 2007, eflornithine is still not accessible in most of Africa, because those countries have been "structurally adjusted" (in the antiseptic terminology of the World Bank), and thus forced to turn their health care systems into user-pay systems. So there's still virtually no eflornithine for sleeping sickness, but even if it happens to be available, most people there can't afford the IV equipment to take the drug anyway.

W Often what's bad about a drug can be turned into something good, if it makes the company money. That's the beauty of the ever-vigilant eye of the marketer, skillful in spotting and exploiting opportunities.

The side effects of SSRI-type antidepressants in

men, particularly delayed ejaculation, are well-known, but no manufacturer as far as I can tell has ever tried to promote its antidepressant drug for this purpose.

In November, 2005, the U.S. Food and Drug Administration told drug maker Johnson & Johnson that its exciting new premature ejaculation (PE) drug, dapoxetine, was "not approvable." J&J maintained that dapoxetine "increased intra-vaginal ejaculatory latency (IEL) time" better than a placebo, and pointed to two 12-week, phase three, randomized, placebo-controlled studies involving about 2,600 men between the ages of 18 and 77. The FDA said there was insuf-ficient data to prove the drug's worth, and sent the company back to the drawing board.

This is just a temporary setback, I'm sure. Dapox-etine, you see, had the financial whiz boys mighty excited, because the potential PE market is not only massive, but also malleable. Could be that as many as 30 to 40 per cent of men are "sufferers" in need of treatment. The market for erectile dysfunction drugs—made so popular by Pfizer's Viagra*—was tiny in comparison, affecting only 10 to 12 per cent of the male population. This is the classic prototype of "selling sickness," where drug makers are helping to invent and shape a new medical condition as a vehicle to tout expensive, newly patented drugs that then sail in to the rescue.

X According to the Therapeutics Initiative at the University of British Columbia, "benzodiazepines may impair functional status by causing confusion, memory loss, dizziness, daytime sleepiness, falls/fractures and depression." This group analyzed the use of benzodiazepines in British Columbia from 1996 to 2002, and found that despite all the possible things that could go wrong, the use continues to grow. In 2002, almost 10 per cent of the population of B.C. (400,000 people) received at least one benzo prescription; of these about 170,000 people are "receiving amounts incompatible with short-term or intermittent use."

Is this really what it seems: likely long-term addiction on a massive scale? One of the most praised books to help with benzodiazepine withdrawal is written by the UK physician, Dr. Heather Ashton, whose manual, *Benzodiazepines: How They Work and How to Withdraw* (revised August, 2002), can be found online at www.benzo.org.uk. The most prescribed benzos include Rivotril* (clonazepam), Ativan* (lorazepam), Serax* (oxazepam), Restoril* (temazepam) and Valium* (diazepam) and of course, Xanax* (alprazolam).

THE FINE PRINT

YMarketing a disease through "disease awareness" campaigns, particularly when there is only one cure, is one way around pesky advertising laws. Therefore, "awareness raising" about nail fungus (onychomycosis) done by Novartis, the makers of Lamisil* (terbinafine), makes some sense, seeing as Lamisil is about the only orally ingested fungus-fighting game in town.

In the Netherlands, Novartis' marketing practices for Lamisil, especially television and print advertisements, came under intense fire, prompting the Dutch Society of General Practitioners to call for a boycott of Novartis. In a letter to the journal of the Royal Dutch Medical Association, *Medisch Contact,* quoted in the *British Medical Journal*, the doctors wrote that nail fungus "rarely requires treatment," and blamed Novartis for having "dollar signs in their eyes, [and] persist[ing] in this undesirable and improper form of advertising."

In the U.S., where drug advertising is legal, Novartis promoted Lamisil with Digger, a scary-looking cartoon character who needs to be tamed with the drug. In 2003, Novartis was ordered by the U.S. FDA's Division of Drug Marketing, Advertising and Communications to withdraw ads featuring Digger, saying that the ads were being "false or misleading because they overstate Lamisil's efficacy, minimize risk information and make an unsubstantiated superiority claim (over other drugs)."

Even so, Lamisil sold over two million prescriptions in the U.S. in 2006, at a cost of over $600 million. In 2001, warning letters were issued by both the U.S. FDA and Health Canada, saying that terbinafine was linked to liver failure and as many as 11 deaths.

Z Bupropion is the generic name for an amphetamine derivative sold under the name Zyban*—for smoking cessation—or Wellbutrin*, when it's used as an antidepressant. Bupropion was introduced in the U.S. in 1985, withdrawn the next year (because it was linked to seizures), and then reintroduced in 1989. Zyban is one of those drugs that have been heavily advertised in Canada, skirting our laws against direct-to-consumer advertising because it can be claimed the marketer it is not actually advertising a drug, but a "disease"—in this case, addiction to nicotine.

Sometimes these ads cross the line. The *Canadian Medical Association Journal* reported that a warning letter from Health Canada to GlaxoSmith-Kline, the maker of Zyban, said their TV ads running just after

New Year's 2000 violated Canadian advertising regulations. They asked Glaxo to "immediately suspend broadcast of these commercials until a full review of this activity can be completed." Instead of removing the ad, the drug maker argued that the ad was legal, calling it "informational programming" by CTV, the network on which it aired. It consisted of a vignette about a successful smoking-cessation experience, followed by a "sponsorship statement." After more back-and-forth between regulator and drug maker, the ad ran for four months, enticing more smokers with the allure of the pill that would help them quit. For its use in smoking-cessation programs, the data on bupropion's effectiveness are not that impressive. After one year, 23 per cent of smokers had been able to quit, compared to 12 per cent taking placebos, which gives patients about a one-in-ten chance that it might work.

The real message is that since Zyban is a drug, the "disease" of smoking gets mongered to sell the cure. In the urge to get us to take products to stop smoking, the other stuff suffers—stuff like the community-based "quit" programs, non-drug approaches to behaviour modification such as acupuncture and other treatments, along with the anti-smoking bylaws and tobacco taxes that have all contributed vastly to getting people to quit an unhealthy habit. Those other things—ones that aren't mongered—may, taken together, go a lot further toward solving society's unhealthy addiction than any magic pill.

EPILOGUE

THIS BOOK DELIVERS A DIAGNOSIS, not a prescription. That's a much taller order. There is no magic pill to treat disease mongering.

We all have to try to make sense of the many factors that arise as an increasingly medicalized society turns more of us into patients. The first thing is to admit we've got a problem.

But most people don't know disease mongering even exists, and health systems managers around the world haven't made serious attempts to rein it in. Where to start?

FIRST, EVERYONE MUST CONSIDER the problem of being on the receiving end of disease-mongering:

→ You may get labelled "sick" and get stuck with the label forever.

→ You may or may not benefit from the medical treatment you're prescribed.

→ You may become anxious about your condition even if the risk of complications is low.

→ You may waste your time and money, and experience side effects of the treatment.

→ In the worst case, you may die from the treatment that is supposed to help you.

NEXT, TAKE A GOOD DOSE of healthy skepticism.

SKEPTICISM IS GOOD FOR YOUR HEALTH. Developing your powers of healthy skepticism about what makes sense means you won't go diving for the new drug or new diagnostic test just because someone thought "it would be good for you." Take time to check out the evidence yourself—including finding out who and what is pushing this medicine now—and never assume that someone else will be doing this for you. The medical system, physicians, pharmacists, regulators and drug companies work under motivations that may be very different from your own.

WHEN IN DOUBT, ASK MORE QUESTIONS, INCLUDING: "WHAT COULD GO WRONG?" If the answer to your questions about a drug's safety is "We don't know," or "We think it's okay," don't assume anything. If there is no warning or information about the safety of a drug or drug combination, that doesn't mean it's safe, appropriate or effective in any given patient. If you want to make a fully informed decision, any test your doctor recommends should be investigated so you understand its potential downsides. You may discover that the test could do more harm than good, cause excess or unnecessary worry (or false optimism), or even lead to a cascade of further tests, investigative procedures, new diagnoses, more cutting, slicing, digging and probing, and so on.

HOW OLD IS THE TREATMENT? If you are given a choice between a drug that has been around for 40 years and one that just went on the market last week, ask for the older one first. Physicians know more about older drugs, including what kinds of serious adverse effects one might expect, and ways to deal with the side effects. Older treatments and drugs come with much more acquired wisdom about how to use them, so you have more knowledge about what you're getting. You must assume that with any new drug the benefits of it could very well be exaggerated and the risks are likely to be either unknown, understated or concealed.

SHARE YOUR REACTIONS. Everyone reacts differently to drugs. An Adverse Drug Reaction (ADR) can be serious, debilitating, or deadly, and generally mean you can't take that drug again. Side effects can be longer term, and are sometimes worth tolerating, if they're alleviating serious symptoms. Sometimes it is the size of the dose that determines whether a drug helps you or hurts you. People who start experiencing strange, troubling, uncomfortable or unusual side effects after starting a drug should suspect it's not their "condition" that's causing it, but it's the drug.

Patients who experience an ADR should immediately report it to their physician or pharmacist, who can file an Adverse Drug Report with Health Canada, or you can file one yourself by phone. Give Health Canada a call at 1-866-234-2345. Operators are standing by.

BIBLIOGRAPHY

Andrist L.C., Arias R.D., Nucatola D., et al. "Women's and providers' attitudes toward menstrual suppression." *Contraception*; Volume 70, Issue 5, Pages 359–363, Nov, 2004.

Ashton, H., *Benzodiazepines: How They Work and How to Withdraw,* revised August 2002. www.benzo.org.uk (accessed 29 November 2007).

Barnard, N., *Neal Barnard's Program for Reversing Diabetes: The Scientifically Proven System for Reversing Diabetes Without Drugs,* Rodale Books, 2006.

Baughman, F., and Hovey, C., *The ADHD Fraud: How Psychiatry Makes "Patients" of Normal Children,* Trafford Publishing, 2006.

Branswell, H., "Giving drug to prevent diabetes no DREAM solution, researchers say," The Canadian Press, Apr. 26, 2007.

Cassels, A., "Manufacturing Patients." Two-part CBC radio documentary, first aired February 4, February 11, 2003.

Cassels, A., "Consumer drug advertising leads to MD backlash in Holland," *CMAJ* • October 1, 2002; 167 (7).

Centre for Medical Consumers, www.medicalconsumers. org (accessed 8 October, 2007).

The Cochrane Collaboration, *The Cochrane Database of Systematic Reviews 2007, Issue 2,* Published by John Wiley and Sons, Ltd. . Cochrane Library: www. cochrane.org

Colagiuri, R., et al, "The Answer to Diabetes Prevention: Science, Surgery, Service Delivery, or Social Policy?" *American Journal of Public Health* 1562–1569 at www.ajph.org, Vol 96, No. 9, September 2006.

Cook J., "Practical guide to medical education." *Pharmaceutical Marketing,* Vol. 6: 14–22., 2001.

Daly, R., and Palmer, K.,"True or false? Women need a form of Viagra" and "Marketing desire; That all depends on who you ask." *Toronto Star,* Dec. 8, 2004.

Espicom Business Intelligence, *Diabetes Drug Discoveries: What the Future Holds,* January, 2007. www.espicom.com

Fortin, C., and Beaulieu, J., *Autopsie d'une catastrophe médicale—L'exemple du Vioxx,* (Éditions de l'Homme, 2005)

Goetz, T., "The Thin Pill," *Wired Magazine*, October 1, 2006.

Goetzl, D., "For SmithKline Beecham, last year's repositioning helped breathe new life into prescription drug Paxil." *Advertising Age,* June 26, 2000.

Graveline, D., *Lipitor: Thief of Memory.* Infinity Publishing. January 28, 2004. His website is at: www.spacedoc.net

Harvard Medical School Family Health Guide at www.health.harvard.edu

Inaugural Conference on Disease Mongering, April 11–13, 2006, Newcastle, Australia, www.diseasemongering.org

The International Network of Cholesterol Skeptics, www.thincs.org

Jefferson T.O., Rivetti D., Di Pietrantonj C., Rivetti A., Demicheli V., "Vaccines for preventing influenza in healthy adults." *Cochrane Database of Systematic Reviews* 1999, Issue 4. Art. No.: CD001269. DOI: 10.1002/14651858.CD001269.pub3.

Kendrick, M., "Should women be offered cholesterol lowering drugs to prevent cardiovascular disease? No." *British Medical Journal*; 334(7601): 983. May 12,2007.

Kendrick, M., *The Great Cholesterol Con: The Truth About What Really Causes Heart Disease and How to Avoid It* (John Blake, 2007).

Kripke, D.F., *The Dark Side of Sleeping Pills.* www.dark-sideofsleepingpills.com, 2006 (accessed 8 October 2006).

Laing, R., Ross-Degnan, D. with the International Network for the Rational Use of Drugs Promoting Rational Drug Use, Training Material. http://dcc2.bumc.bu.edu/prdu/default.html (accessed 8 October 2007).

Lane, C., *Shyness: How Normal Behavior Became a Sickness,* (Yale University Press, 2007).

Lippman A, Melnychuk R, Shimmin C, Boscoe M. "Human papillomavirus, vaccines and women's health: questions and cautions." *Canadian Medical Association Journal,* 177(5): 484, August 28, 2007.

McNeil, Donald, "Cosmetic Saves a Cure for Sleeping Sickness," *New York Times,* February 9, 2001

Medawar C, Hardon A: *Medicines out of Control?—Antidepressants and the Conspiracy of Goodwill.* Aksant Academic Publishers, 2004.

Moynihan, R., "Scientists find new disease: motivational deficiency disorder." *British Medical Journal,* 2006; 332:745, 1 April, 2006 (accessed 8 Oct 2007).

Médecins Sans Frontièrs' Drugs for Neglected Diseases Initiative, www.accessmed-msf.org/dndi.asp (accessed 8 October, 2007).

Moynihan, R. and Cassels, A., *Selling Sickness: How the World's Biggest Pharmaceutical Companies are Turning us all into Patients,* GreyStone Books, 2005.

National Vaccine Information Centre at: www.nvic.org (accessed 8 October, 2007)

Norris SL, Zhang X, Avenell A, Gregg E, Schmid CH, Lau J. "Long-term nonpharmacological weight loss interventions for adults with prediabetes" [Cochrane review]. In: *Cochrane Database of Systematic Reviews 2005 Issue 2.* Chichester (UK): John Wiley & Sons, Ltd; 2005.

OneWorldHealth, www.oneworldhealth.org (accessed 8 October, 2007).

O'Reilly, J., "An Eye for an Eye: Foresight on Remedies of LASIK Surgery's Problems" *University of Cincinnati Law Review,* Winter 2002.

The Pharmaceutical Journal, Patient-Oriented Evidence that Matters (POEM) entitled: "Treating prediabetes does not affect progression," published in Vol 278 No 7435 p66 20 January 2007. POEMs are found at www.pjonline.com/noticeboard/series/poem.html (accessed 8 October 2007).

PLoS Medicine, various authors. A Collection of articles on Disease Mongering, Public Library of Science, collections.plos.org/plosmedicine/diseasemongering-2006.php (accessed 8 October, 2007).

Rako, S., *No More Periods?: The Risks of Menstrual Suppression and Other Cutting-Edge Issues About Hormones and Women's Health.* Harmony, 2003.

Ravnskov, U., *The Cholesterol Myths.* New Trends Publishing, 2000.

Romain, J., *Knock, ou le triomphe de la médecine.* Gallimard, 1924.

Sanson, G., *The Myth of Osteoporosis: What every woman should know about creating bone health.* MCD Century Publications, 2003.

Santaguida PL, Balion C, Hunt D, Morrison K, Gerstein H, Raina P. *Diagnosis, prognosis, and treatment of impaired glucose tolerance and impaired fasting glucose* [Evidence Report/Technology Assessment no 128]. Rockville (MD): Agency for Healthcare Research and Quality; 2005. www.ahrq.gov/downloads/pub/evidence/pdf/impglucose/impglucose.pdf (accessed 8 October, 2007).

Schachter HM, Pham B, King J, Langford S, Moher D. "How efficacious and safe is short-acting methylphenidate for the treatment of attention-deficit disorder in children and adolescents? A meta-analysis." *CMAJ* 2001;165(11):1475–88. www.cmaj.ca/cgi/content/abstract/165/11/1475

Seaman, B., *The Greatest Experiment Ever Performed on Women: Exploding the Estrogen Myth.* Hyperion Books, 2003.

Sheldon, T., "Dutch GPs call for ban on Novartis products" BMJ 2002: 325:355.

Silversides, A."Direct-to-consumer prescription drug ads getting bolder" *CMAJ,* August 21, 2001; 165 (4).

Social Audit, www.socialaudit.org.uk (accessed 8 October, 2007).

Therapeutics Initiative, "Mild Hypertension—An approach to using evidence in the decision making process," *Therapeutics Letter,* issue 62, January—February 2007 at www.ti.ubc.ca/node/36 (accessed 8 October, 2007).

Therapeutics Initiative, "Use of Benzodiazepines in BC—Is it consistent with recommendations?" *Therapeutics Letter,* issue 54, November-December 2004. www.ti.ubc.ca/node/46, (accessed 25 October, 2007).

Tonks, A., "Withdrawal from paroxetine can be severe, warns FDA." *British Medical Journal* 324:260. 2 February 2002.

The University of Toronto Centre for Evidence-based Medicine, www.cebm.utoronto.ca (accessed 8 October, 2007).

United States Food and Drug Administration Center for Devices and Radiological Health, www.fda.gov/cdrh (accessed 8 October, 2007).

Vision Surgery Rehab Network, www.visionsurgeryrehab.org (accessed 8 October, 2007).

Welch, H.G., *Should I be Tested for Cancer: Maybe Not and Here's Why.* University of California Press, 2004.

Wells GA, Cranney A, Boucher M, Peterson J, Shea B, Robinson V, et al. "Bisphosphonates for the primary and secondary prevention of osteoporotic fractures in postmenopausal women: a meta-analysis" [Technology report]. Ottawa: Canadian Agency for Drugs and Technologies in Health, 2006. www.cadth.ca/index.php/en/hta/reports-publications/search/publication/659; (accessed 8 October, 2007.

Wesensten, N., et al, "Maintaining alertness and performance during sleep deprivation: modafinil versus caffeine." *Psychopharmacology (Berl)* 2002 Jan;159(3):238–47.

Woloshin, S., and Schwartz, L., "Giving Legs to Restless Legs: A Case Study of How the Media Helps Make People Sick." *PLoS Med* 3(4): e170. 2006—www.pubmedcentral.nih.gov/articlerender.fcgi?artid=1434499 (accessed 8 October, 2007).

World Health Organization, *Promoting Rational Drug Use,* Training Material, dcc2.bumc.bu.edu/prdu/default.html

ACKNOWLEDGEMENTS

THERE'S NOTHING LIKE HAVING A FRIEND with a printing press in his basement who lulls you with an easy promise of producing a book and then holds you to your pledge to make that book happen. It helps hugely if that same person has a poet for a wife who edits like a ring and a bell, and she has a brother who is a talented artist with a freshly twisted sense of how the world fits together. So first of all, many thanks to Marc, Alisa and Jeremy, without whom this project would never have been conceived of, illustrated, poeticized, launched, or delivered. Special thanks to Jeremy for his outstanding drawings, and Alisa for coming up with the idea that the text should be poetry and then making sure that happened.

AN EXTRA SPECIAL THANKS to Don Husereau who worked his magic on the content of this book and Andrew MacLeod who supplied numerous helpful signposts along the way. Many other people gave loads of thoughtful comments, written feedback, sharp critiques, and showed a high level of respect for me by delivering the occasional smack to the head when I needed it. These people include Wendy Armstrong, Warren Bell, David Blair, James McCormack, Dave Clements,

Christine Dunsmoor, Colleen Fuller, Andrea Gregg, Eleanor Kallio, Heather-Ann Laird, Joel Lexchin, Martin Lind, Janice McNary, Kathleen O'Grady, Catherine Oliver, Cheryl Pardue, Kerry Patriarche, Alicia Priest, Suzanne Slater, Lois Stewart , Chad Vandermolen, and Rebecca Warburton.

I'D ALSO LIKE TO USE THIS OPPORTUNITY to remind professors in the English Department at the Royal Military College of Canada that this book is living proof that their real job is to turn out literate officers to lead Canada's military, not pseudo-poets. And finally, hugs and thanks to Lynda, Morgan and Chase for tolerating yet another project.

Photo: Earla Legault, Harrison Hot Springs, BC.

ALAN CASSELS is a healthcare policy researcher, and co-author of the international bestseller *Selling Sickness: How the World's Biggest Pharmaceutical Companies are Turning Us All into Patients* (GreyStone 2005). He lives in Victoria, BC.